THE MIDNIGHT BLUES

SANVI VAIDYA

ISBN 979-888521412-4

From my atoms, to yours.

Contents

Contents

"HE NOT BUSY LIVING, IS BUSY DYING"
~ BOB DYLAN

The Midnight Blues

by

SANVI VAIDYA

"IT IS BECAUSE YOU WERE OUT THERE TO FIND,
YOU WERE FOUND."~ SANVI

Table Of Contents

- ACKNOWLEDGEMENTS
- FOREWORD
- PREFACE
- PROLOGUE

VOLUME 001 :- DOWN THE RABBIT HOLE

1. Pretty much sucks
2. Let's be grateful for the good
3. Space and Love - 1
4. Space and Love - 2

TABLE OF CONTENTS

VOLUME 002 :- THE FOLK - TALES

TABLE OF CONTENTS

Acknowledgements

A big thankyou to all my fellow readers of webnovel, for all your support and encouragement throughout the course of the book.

To, BTS(the korean band/Bangtan Boys)which is not only a music band, but also a family for me. They have been my biggest inspiration, ever since I have known them. Their thoughts and opinions have helped me get out of hard times and get back on track with life. That being yourself is necessary. It takes time to move on from the need of social validation, but when you do so and when you learn to accept yourself with the good and the bad; appreciate yourself with all your might, then there is nothing more empowering.

"THE MIDNIGHT BLUES", would not have been possible, if not for you all.

Preface

With this virus outbreak,

    And all lives at stake,

    We now realise,

    And try to be a little wise..

    About the deeds that we've done,

    The promises, that were left broken.

    Our ruthless hearts that never hesitated , to slaughter any wild.

    To rip apart the poor child.

    Our polluted minds that went way too blind, to see the scarce green.

    To sense the upcoming ending.

    We kept clinging onto the nature's fruits,

    Forgetting to water the burning roots.

    Now that we have to repay in tons,

    Again been shown that we are just mere humans.

A lot has happened since the Covid outbreak. In these two years of pandemic, we lost our loved ones, our livelihoods, the mental peace, physical health, our sanity. We lost so much, in so less time. It took a harsh toll on our mental health. The lockdown, the loneliness, the fear of not knowing what bizzare thing we would have to face next. Our lives started sounding like a tragic novel. It became a tragic novel for quite a long time.

In the admist of all this chaos, one realisation that hit me very hard, was that , the Life Goes On. That we do not stop existing. That no matter what tragedy happens with us, we won't cease to exist. We still have our lives ahead. People went through a lot of trauma, loss, fear, anxiety, depression, anger and then acceptance. People fought their way through and out of the hell hole. We clawed our way back in. We grew around the trauma, we grew big and strong. We learnt new things and we learnt some old things for a very first time. We kept ourselves occupied, we brainstormed, came up with various ways to do so. We grew more patient towards the surroundings, towards ourselves. Us humans, what we know, is to survive. That is our basic instinct.

Life is no walk in the park. It gets ugly at times, but it teaches us to thrive, to clench onto the bare minimum, it gets us through the nerve- chilling nights and makes us hope for a summer sky.

When will it all go back to normal? We ask ourselves . The answer is, it won't. What is normal anyways? Everyone has a different version of the normal, and it keeps changing from time to time.

❧❧❧

(I started "The Midnight Blues", somewhere around the May of 2019.)

Audrea is a seventeen year old girl, living in San Francisco, California. She lives with her loving parents and has a amazing group of friends. Her love for maintaining journals, is never dying. Maintaining a diary feels like a lot of work and a lot of commitment to her. The obligation of writing something everyday. She is definetly not a diary person. There are days when she writes a lot, writes her heart out and there are these time frames where she doesn't write at all. Like at times a wave of motivation hits her, out of the blue and sometimes for a brief period of time, her mind seems like the Sahara. What she writes in the journals is particular incidences of her life. One's that are stuck in her head for good and for bad. She writes about people. Audrea thinks that it is interesting how our individual behaviors are hugely imapacted by what we see people do around us and how we percieve that, react to that and how we adapt certain things out of it. It is fascinating how all of us are same yet different, unique in our own way. Audrea knows that art is 'subjective'. There is no such thing as being the best at it or beating someone up to it. She knows that we have to improve on an individual basis, at our own pace. This understanding, reflects vividly through her writings.

"It is okay to quit, but not on yourself."

VOLUME 001

DOWN THE RABBIT HOLE

1. ~pretty much sucks

"If it isn't scary, it isn't the reality."
I was breathing heavily, my vision was blurred. I could hear sirens blaring in distance. There were three ambulances, the paramedics and some cops as I vaguely remember. They lifted me up, I was bleeding, I tried to speak up but before I could say anything I just blacked out. I woke up to my mom resting her head on my hand , dad was sleeping on a couch in the room and I had a oxygen mask on. I was in the hospital.
"Mom.." I blurted out. "Oh honey, you are awake..oh Hans, sweetie Audrea's awake!" She stroked my cheeks with happy tears in her eyes and dad held my hand kissing my forehead.
"How are you feeling Audrea? Are you in a lot of pain?" dad asked , giving me a concerned look.
"No..but where are gammy and pappy? Are they okay?" I was really worried about my grandparents.
"They are undergoing treatments, I'm sure they'll be okay. Don't worry, nothing would happen to them", mom said reassuring me.
I was in the hospital for a few more days. Whenever I asked my parents about gammy and pappy, they would just give random answers. They were freaking me out, to be honest; but I decided not to loose my hopes. Eventually I recovered and got home.

"Are you going to tell me what's happening to gammy and pappy? Why aren't they home with us? Are they okay? Why won't you tell me anything?!", I snapped.

"Honey, come here sit down" , mom let out a sigh.

"I'm sorry sweetie, but we were concerned about you, your health." dad sat next to me.

"What? What is it ?! Tell me please!" I was starting to panic. That's when I came to know that my grandparents were no more . That they passed away the day before. I stood up and started yelling at my parents for not telling me, I screamed and cried my heart out. Then I just went numb, everything around me stopped for a moment. I couldn't feel my legs and I collapsed. Mom-Dad tried gathering me but I couldn't feel anything, I had no strength left. I couldn't breathe, my entire childhood just flashed infront of my eyes. All the happy times with gammy and pappy , their smiling faces..now the smiles all faded away and it became all grey. As if the blue of my sky got drained out and now, it seemed so dark, so lifeless. It felt like I've fallen into a deep pit filled with darkness and not a star of hope hovered above the dreary sky. I couldn't even cry, I just sat there staring into the nothingness.

• It was during the holidays. I spent the Thanksgiving and Christmas with my all time favourites, my gammy and pappy at Florida. The goofily decorated Christmas tree and all the gifts, the cookies and cakes ; it felt like I was 5 again. Mom and dad were going to join us for New year, but mom got caught up into some urgent charity work and so instead, pappy decided to drive us all the way to San Francisco. Pappy just loved the good old

road trips, he was so excited. We got on the road two days before the 31ˢᵗ. It was snowing heavily and was bit of a haze everywhere. I had snuggled up in the backseat with my blanket and gammy and pappy were singing the, "Last Christmas" with glee. I just fell asleep to their melodious voices. Suddenly I felt a jerk and the car just swirled and we crashed into the woods. I got thrown out of the car and hit the grounds so hard, that went all dizzy. I felt a throbbing pain all over I'm in my body , I reached out to the phone in my pocket and somehow managed to call 911. I don't remember anything after that.

• It's been more than two years now. I'm going to be 18 in a few months, adult as they say; but there hasn't been a single day where I haven't thought about them . For a couple of months after the accident, I'd get nightmares about it and I cried myself to sleep every other day. I miss them so much . Life is not easy at all. It's a jigsaw puzzle, you put the right piece, you are all set but if don't , then you are just screwed. They say everything happens for it's own good. I don't know what good comes out of such tragic incidents, where people loose their loved ones. Although I know one thing for sure that though my grandparents aren't with me anymore, they'll always be there . I have their beautiful memories and the souvenirs; and I know they won't be happy to see me drown myself in all the sadness. I know it's hard to get out of this, but it's necessary. They were good people and didn't deserve such a horrific end, but sometimes we just can't have all the answers. No matter how much hard we try , we can't escape fate. The only thing that keeps me sane, is that the

last time I saw my grandparents, was not in a terrible state. I saw them singing Christmas songs , looking into eachother's eyes and being happy and grateful for everything. I bid farewell to their happy faces and that's how I'm going to remember them .
• Now every Christmas, I sit near the fireplace with mom and dad. I wear the red bow with reindeers on it that gammy gave me on my last Christmas at their place; and I sing. I sing "Last Christmas" through the bottom of my heart and picture gammy and pappy's smiling face. I embrace what's good.

Enter Caption

2. ~let's be grateful for the good

Be grateful, for what you have ; not because others can't have it.
Be grateful, for you get food on your plate whenever you are
hungry; not because others are starving to death.
Be grateful for having a shelter above your head; not because
others sleep drenched wet in the rain by a footpath.
Be grateful for the things you can afford, not because others can't
even have the bare minimum.

We often tend to tell our loved to be grateful for leading such luxurious lives and we console them by saying that many people around us are still struggling to survive. But, how can we be comforted by knowing that someone out there is suffering? It's disturbing how people tend to achieve a sense of relief by looking down upon those who are in need.

Enter Caption

My mom, runs an NGO "The helping hand" for orphans and all the kids in need . Many a times I accompany mom to work. The very first time I went there, I was 6years old. It was my birthday and mom told me that it would be a great idea to celebrate it with the kids. Although, I wanted to have a party in our backyard with my school friends and play with them all day long; but mom told me to invite them to the shelter home instead. She assured me that it will be fun. I was a bit unhappy but I didn't argue further. The day after that we went there with my birthday cake and treats and chocolates and lots of toys .

While in the car , on our way to the home, I asked mom, "mom, why can't we just have the party in our backyard? I don't even know these kids. "

"Sweetie, unlike you these kids haven't got their mom and dad around them. They don't have a home, or a family. Now that they stay here we help find them good parents, who would love them tremendously and take good care of them. They also deserve to be loved and to be happy. Until then , shouldn't we share our happiness with them? Because when we share our happiness?",
mom looked at me.

"It doubles up!", I exclaimed.

Dad looked behind and smiled and mom booped me on my nose. When we arrived at the shelter home, there were kids playing in the front yard, giggling and running all over the lush green grass. My parents went in to arrange everything in the hall and told me to hangout with the kids outside. I took a look around and saw a girl my age sitting on one of the swings . She was wearing a cute red dress with little white hearts on it, and she had a red bow . She didn't look very sad, so I went over and sat on the swing next to hers.

"Hi, I am Audrea." She looked up and gave me a weak smile.

"I am Bree. Are you going to live with us?", she wondered.

"No, actually today, it is my birthday today, so we are going to celebrate it here. How do you celebrate your birthday?", I asked

her.

"I use to celebrate it with my parents too, when I was with them . They died last month in a car accident. I live here since then, now I just have a little cupcake and play with the rest of the kids on my birthday.",she sighed.

"I'm sorry for your loss. When is your birthday though?".

"It's today.",she said looking down at the grass, twirling a little flower between her fingers.

I felt really bad for her, I didn't want her to be sad on her birthday.

"You know, you could cut the cake with me. Afterall we are birthday twins." She looked up at me and her face lit up.

"Really?",she asked me with a twinkle in her eyes.

"Yes! Friends?", I lend my hand for a shake; she hugged me tight and gently placed her flower in my hair. Then we played for a while and ran all over, holding hands and laughing out loud. I was so happy. This was so much better than a birthday party in my backyard. Mom- dad called us all in , they had decorated the hall beautifully. It looked magical and there was my cake on the table in the centre. There were treats , chocolates and lots of gifts in a corner. I walked upto my parents and told them about Bree. They happily agreed and gave me kisses on my cheeks. Then Bree and I cut the cake together, everyone was singing happy birthday and clapping for us, all happy faces; the room was filled with giggles and laughter.

I looked at Bree, she was the happiest amongst all of us; had a grin left to right that lit up the whole room. Looking at her smile goofily at me, made me grin too. I was so happy, this was the best birthday ever! We had the cake and treats, then we opened all the gifts. I let her keep half of them . We also bought toys for the other kids , everyone had a great time. While bidding them goodbye, I felt sad. I didn't want to leave, Bree and I were still holding hands and chatting with eachother.

"Thankyou very much.", she said with warm eyes, tears gathering up in the corners.

"No, don't say thankyou. Friends do such things for eachother all the time. I promise I'll come visit you often." We hugged and said goodbye.

I went to see her every weekend with mom. We used to talk, play and have lots of fun. After a year, she was adopted by a wonderful couple who lived a couple of blocks away from us; Mr. and Mrs. Adams. We started to hangout regularly then , and went to the same highschool. Eventually Bree and I became bestfriends ; and we still are by eachother's side. She is like those people who are always happy and optimistic and smile their way through hard times. When my grandparents died she never left my side for the entire week. She's the one of the bestest people in my life, she is my sunshine and I am very grateful to have her. I could not ask for anything more.

3. ~space and love - 1

If you ask me how exactly I define love ; then you must be ready to understand my version of the definition. Everyone around us has got tangled into different definitions of love, because it keeps on changing from person to person. Although, I'm glad to be coming across one such love letter that changed my whole perspective towards love and relationships completely. One of the Lemony Snicket's "Love letters to Beatrice", is how I now define love. I believe in it with all my heart and soul. It'll make you chuckle and giggle in the beginning and give you a soft smile in between but towards the end I'm sure it will give you much more than just a definition. It will not only warm your eyes but also your heart. So, hear it goes...

{Do you love me?

"I will love you with no regard to the actions of our enemies or the jealousies of actors. I will love you with no regard to the outrage of certain parents or the boredom of certain friends. I will love you no matter what is served in the world's cafeterias or what game is played at each and every recess. I will love you no matter how many fire drills we are all forced to endure, and no matter what is drawn upon the blackboard in a blurring, boring chalk. I will love you no matter how many mistakes I make when trying to reduce fractions, and no matter how difficult it is

to memorize the periodic table. I will love you no matter what your locker combination was, or how you decided to spend your time during study hall. I will love you no matter how your soccer team performed in the tournament or how many stains I received on my cheerleading uniform. I will love you if I never see you again, and I will love you if I see you every Tuesday. I will love you if you cut your hair and I will love you if you cut the hair of others. I will love you if you abandon your baticeering, and I will love you if you retire from the theater to take up some other, less dangerous occupation. I will love you if you drop your raincoat on the floor instead of hanging it up and I will love you if you betray your father. I will love you even if you announce that the poetry of Edgar Guest is the best in the world and even if you announce that the work of Zilpha Keatley Snyder is unbearably tedious. I will love you if you abandon the theremin and take up the harmonica and I will love you if you donate your marmosets to the zoo and your tree frogs to M. I will love you as the starfish loves a coral reef and as kudzu loves trees, even if the oceans turn to sawdust and the trees fall in the forest without anyone around to hear them. I will love you as the pesto loves the fetuccini and as the horseradish loves the miyagi, as the tempura loves the ikura and the pepperoni loves the pizza. I will love you as the manatee loves the head of lettuce and as the dark spot loves the leopard, as the leech loves the ankle of a wader and as a corpse loves the beak of the vulture. I will love you as the doctor loves his sickest patient and a lake loves its thirstiest swimmer. I will love you as the beard loves the chin, and the crumbs love the beard, and the damp napkin loves the crumbs, and the precious document loves the dampness in the napkin, and the squinting eye of the reader loves the smudged print of the document, and the tears of sadness love the squinting eye as it misreads what is written. I will love you as the iceberg loves the ship, and the passengers love the lifeboat, and the lifeboat loves the teeth of the sperm whale, and the sperm whale loves the flavor of naval uniforms. I will love you as a child loves to overhear the conversations of its parents, and the parents love the sound of their own arguing voices, and as the pen loves to write down the words these voices utter in a notebook for safekeeping. I will love you as a shingle loves falling off a house on a windy day and striking a grumpy person across the chin, and as an oven loves malfunctioning in the middle of roasting a turkey. I will love you as an airplane loves to fall from a clear blue sky and as an escalator loves to entangle expensive scarves in its mechanisms. I will love you as a wet paper towel loves to be crumpled into a ball and thrown at a bathroom ceiling and an eraser loves to leave dust in the hairdos of the people who talk too much. I will love you as a cufflink loves to drop from its shirt and explore the party for itself and as a pair of white gloves loves to slip delicately into the punchbowl. I will love you as a taxi loves the muddy splash of a puddle and as a library loves the patient tick of a clock. I will love you as a thief loves a gallery and as a crow loves a murder, as a cloud loves bats and as a range loves braes. I will love you as misfortune loves orphans, as fire loves innocence and as justice loves to sit and watch while everything goes wrong. I will love you as a battlefield loves young men and as peppermints love your allergies, and I will love you as the banana peel loves the shoe of a man who was just struck by a shingle falling off a house. I will love you as a volunteer fire department loves rushing into burning buildings and as burning buildings love to chase them back out, and as a parachute loves to leave a blimp and as a blimp operator loves to chase after it. I will love you as a dagger loves a certain person's back, and as a certain person loves to wear daggerproof tunics, and as a daggerproof tunic loves to go to a certain dry cleaning facility, and how a certain employee of a dry cleaning facility loves to stay up late with a pair of binoculars, watching a dagger factory for hours in the hopes of catching a burglar, and as a burglar loves sneaking up behind people with binoculars, suddenly realizing that she has left her dagger at home. I will love you as a drawer loves a secret compartment, and as a secret compartment loves a secret, and as a secret loves to make a person gasp, and as a gasping person loves a glass of brandy to calm their nerves, and as a glass of brandy loves to shatter on the floor, and as the noise of glass shattering loves to make someone else gasp, and as someone else gasping loves a nearby desk to lean against, even if leaning against it presses a lever that loves to open a drawer and reveal a secret compartment. I will love you until all such compartments are discovered and opened, and until all the secrets have gone gasping into the world. I will love you until all the codes and hearts have been broken and until every anagram and egg has been unscrambled. I will love you until every fire is extinguished and until every home is rebuilt form the handsomest and most susceptible of woods, and until every criminal is handcuffed by the laziest of policemen. I will love you until M. hates snakes and J. hates grammar, and I will love you until C. realizes S. is not worthy of his love and N. realizes he is not worthy of the V. I will love you until the bird hates a nest and the worm hates an apple, and until the apple hates a tree and the tree hates a nest, and until a bird hates a tree and an apple hates a nest, although honestly I cannot imagine that last occurrence no matter how hard I try. I will love you as we grow older, which has just happened, and has happened again, and happened several days ago, continuously, and then several years before that, and will continue to happen as the spinning hands of every clock and the flipping pages of every calendar mark the passage of time, except for the clocks that people have forgotten to wind and the calendars that people have forgotten to place in a highly visible area. I will love you as we find ourselves farther and farther from one another, where once we were so close that we could slip the curved straw, and the long, slender spoon, between our lips and fingers respectively. I will love you until the chances of us running into one another slip from skim to zero, and until your face is fogged by distant memory, and your memory faced by distant fog, and your fog memorized by a distant face, and your distance distanced by the memorized memory of a foggy fog. I will love you no matter where you go and who you see, no matter where you avoid and who you don't see, and no matter who sees you avoiding where you go. I will

love you no matter what happens to you, and no matter how I discover what happens to you, and no matter what happens to me as I discover this, and no matter how I am discovered after what happens to me happens to me as I am discovering this. I will love you if you don't marry me. I will love you if you marry someone else — your co-star, perhaps, or Y., or even O., or anyone Z. through A., even R. although sadly I believe it will be quite some time before two women can be allowed to marry — and I will love you if you have a child, and I will love you if you have two children, or three children, or even more, although I personally think three is plenty, and I will love you if you never marry at all, and never have children, and spend your years wishing you had married me after all, and I must say that on late, cold nights I prefer this scenario out of all the scenarios I have mentioned. That, Beatrice, is how I will love you even as the world goes on its wicked way."
By Lemony Snicket.}

4. ~space and love - 2

I like to feel your eyes on me, when I look away.
I like my safe space in your arms, on all of the days, good or bad.
I like how the linen sheets now smell like you. I like, l like how I
wake up to the sight of you peacefully resting your head on my
palm; calmly wondering in a far fetched dreamland.
And I see..I peek in your dreams and I'm delighted to see us .
Holding hands and walking down a country lane sharing the
talkative silences; and the time's caught in still.
I caress you hair and stroke your cheeks, planting a little kiss on
your lips. You smile unknowingly and pull me closer, into your
arms. Oh I feel so loved.

{I send you all the thankes which my heart can conceive, or my
words can rehearse. For your many travailes and care taken for
me, my debt to you is not less, but pay it i never shall in this
world}
- Thou shall live forever in my verse~
I remember thy charismatic physique and thy tranquil gaze,
For I can go for an eternity, singing thy praise.
I can breathe thou in the air, for thy scent is purely amaze,
It leaves my world baptized and rebirthed by it's liquid grace.

In the moment when I saw thee for the very first time, I recall no
sense of consciense...
For my heart skipped a beat, and my ballad skipped a rhyme...
I am always concious to thee, for thy presence never leaves me,
For all I refuse and thee i choose.
My words is my only way to converse,
For I solemnly assure thee, my beloved,
Until the very end, thou shall forever live in my verse.

Isn't everything that we all do is to be a little more loved and
wanted ? Isn't it all for love at the end? And the energy, "the god"
some may call it...is nothing but this space . This space between
us. Holding us together, for once and forever.

• Kai Menken

I met Kai, during the annual carnival. Highschool was about to
start after the carnival. Two days were left for the carnival to
end. Me and Bree used to go to the fair almost everyday. We even
set up our own little stall of handmade jewellery and art pieces
at the fair; it was right next to Mrs. Carney's Delicious Donuts.
She was a wonderful women, infact she helped us getting many
customers. She lived next door to Bree , with her husband Aiden
and eight years old son, Liam. Liam was such a good kid, oh
and when he used to smile , his eyes would just disappear. He
was adorable. Infact their whole family was very warm and

welcoming.

It was the second last day of the fair. Bree and I had set up our stall ; playing some music we entertained ourselves, while waiting for the customers.

"Um hey excuse me?" , a really sweet voice called us.

That's when I saw Kai for the first time. He was tall, with broad shoulders and had chiseled jawline with a cute dimple on his right cheek. His eyes were hazel with a tint of light brown; he had wavy hair and wore square-framed glasses. He was wearing a white t-shirt that embraced his hard chest , a shirt over it and denim jeans paired up with cool painted sneakers. I completely zoned out for a moment ; and I must tell you this happens very rare. He just stood there looking at me , as if he was trying to hear my thoughts. We zoned back in reality as Bree cleared her throat on purpose.

"Hey, hi umm hello umm so what would you like to buy?" , I was totally embarrassing myself but not like I haven't done it before duh.

He chuckled softly and said that he wanted to buy a nice painting for his house and a bracelet spelling out 'Joonie' for his little sister.

"Oh how so sweet, let me just make the bracelet and Audrea would you show him the paintings please?", saying this Bree winked at me.

What can say, she was one hell of a person afterall ! I let Kai inside the stall to take a better look at the paintings.

"So, what do you think? " I asked.

"Well, I would be lying if I say that I don't want to buy the all. All the paintings are really aesthetic and the beautiful quotes , musings at random corners make them even more meaningful. As if they bring them to life. ", Kai said looking straight into my eyes and I almost drowned into his.

"That was one hell of a compliment. ", I thought to myself.

"Thankyou very much! I'm glad you like them." I said getting a bit nervous; because I'm so not good at handling compliments, I just can not.

"Are you kidding me? I love them . You made all these?" I nodded yes.

" Wow , I wish I was this talented. " , he said with a twinkle in his eyes and I grinned left to right.

"I would take um, this. " , he said holding the one where I painted a masquerade ball.

I packed it carefully and handed it over with the bracelet. He thanked me and Bree and left. I looked at and Bree and I almost squealed.

5. ~space and love - 3

Enter Caption

It was the last day of carnival. Bree and I had decided to packup the stall early and enjoy the evening. We made a fair amount of money out of our little stall. So we went to the mall , tried numerous outfits, bought some of them and ate our favourite, brownie with ice-cream waffles. Since it was the last day of carnival, we wanted to dress up a little and were gonna meet our friends; Amber, Daniel, Ara, Eleanor and Neo. I was with them since elementary school and now they became good friends with Bree too. We all made one heck of a group.

I wore a rainbow tank top, black leather jacket with ripped denims and my boots to compliment the look. Styled my hair into cute space buns and then my favourite coffee brown lipstick to go. Dressing up and hanging out with my friends was the best thing. As decided, we all met up at the carnival fair by 7 o'clock.

We went on many rides, took lots of pictures, had lots of junk food. Bree had a family dinner so she went home early. Everyone else went home too; but I wanted to have a last ride on the Ferris wheel so I bid goodbye to them. I sat on the Ferris wheel and next to me was Kai ; yeah the dreamy guy. I didn't see him before I hopped in.

"Hey, Audrea right?" , oh he remembered.

"Yeah , what's your name?", I asked.

"Kai, Kai Menken. "

Wow his name itself was so charming. The Ferris wheel started.

Kai and his family had moved to North Beach a couple of weeks ago and he was coming to the 'North Beach High' for highschool. I was excited, for we were going to be in the same highschool and probably the same class if luck was by my side. That day we were on the Ferris wheel for almost half an hour, just talking about random things, sharing embarassing moments and getting to know eachother. Then we went to the photobooth and clicked tons of pictures. Though I had known Kai for just a couple of hours, he seemed very familiar and welcoming. He gave me butterflies everytime he smiled at me , he was the sweetest guy I ever came across. He was so polite and adorable, oh how could anyone not have a crush on him.

Eventually highschool started and luckily he was in four of my classes. We used to hangout quite often and he became a part of our group in no time. He was nice to everyone and most of the girls in highschool had a crush on him. It was hard to see them flirt with him, but he never gave in much. Kai used to come over for studies sometimes; I helped him in science and he helped me in mathematics. We were such nerds, but it was really great, getting to know him a little better by each passing day. I didn't know him from my childhood but how much ever I did since we met, I liked it all. Kai was an amazing guy and I knew that he liked me too; because we girls, we always know. Am I right or am I right? But still I was nervous to ask him out. He didn't ask me either, so I wondered many a times if it all was just in my head.

It wasn't.

The next year during carnival, when our group went to the fair, Kai took me on a Ferris wheel ride . We were at the top when it stopped, apparently he had begged the Ferris wheel guy to do so. He took my hands into his and said,

"I love you Audrea. You are the most wonderful girl I've ever met. You are so beautiful that whenever I see you, I'm left with no words. Your smile lits up the whole room and it makes my heart smile too. Your laugh gives me butterflies and whenever you look at me my heart skips a beat. Yeah you are a bit weird but weird in the most amazing way possible. You are my type of weird. Whenever you talk passionately about things, your eyes shine with glee and I could listen to you, like forever. I couldn't help but fall head over heels, who wouldn't I mean.", he chuckled softly.

"I love you Audrea I really do."

I was left in an awe.

"And I love you Kai, infact I never stopped loving you.", happy tears rolled down my cheeks.

He brushed them off gently and stroked my cheeks and placed his lips on mine. His lips were so soft and warm and the whole moment was mesmerizing. Our friends cheered from the ground and the Ferris wheel started again. Kai held my hand and our fingers entwined as we watched the sunset, riding the Ferris wheel. Kai, being my side made the sunset even more special. When we got down we had a group hug and Bree cried happy tears too.She was so happy seeing me happy; my bestfriend afterall. All of us then had fun with the rides , photobooth and went for karaoke.

Kai walked me home and kissed me goodbye. I had the biggest smile on my face. The entire evening was so magical; love was in the air. Since then Kai and I have been together. We've been through the perks and troughs of life but never left eachother's side and the Ferris wheel, has always remained our happy place.

6. ~brevity is the soul of wit

I write because I'm good friends with words,
Long since my childhood they have been with me through all my
thick and thin.
Through my summers and my winters, through my spring and
my autumns.
Not that the others are strangers,
Neither the canvases betrayed me
Nor that the lenses left my side...
But still , they are not more than acquaintances.
I write...
I write because I feel as a whole
My words, like a puzzle piece; complete me.
They stand for me , they talk for me.
When everyone leaves, they stay...
They have always stayed to uphold me.
When it feels like the end, and everything fades away...
I'm left with my words,
My statements and lines.
My poems and stories.
My rants and letters.

You see, I'm an introvert and it's very hard for me to express myself openly. There was a time, when it was hard for me to express myself at all. I have major trust issues and I felt that sharing your problems with others would just add on to their problems and that it will burden them . Although, I know better now. Expressing yourself to others and sharing how feel with others won't burden them with anything. It will give you relief and make them feel worthy. The right ones, would not run away. They will be happy to be your safe place.

I started to write poems and stories when I was eight; being very shy as a kid I used to write a lot. Writing down my feelings, gave me happiness. My diary was my very first friend, one who would never judge me but will always be there to listen when I pour my heart out. A very wise woman once told me that, there would be times when I may feel very lonely between people and won't be able to figure what I want. At these times, I'd find home in my words, in my writings. When everything around me gets darker and the reality starts to bite, I tend to write stories and create characters and weave a beautiful, happy story with my words. I'd give it a happy ending, though I know that not all stories have a happy ending; and the ones that do, aren't really endings; but we read, to escape from the bitter reality don't we? So, why not fill the stories with happiness and laughter and let it's end give the keen reader a sign of contentment and fill his/her world with sparkles, though it maybe for a couple of minutes. These good hours that he/she would invest in a good read would leave a little smile on their everyday gloomy faces.

After reading the whole series of Harry Potter I was aspired to be one of their kind. I even put the protective charms outside my room, to keep away all the evil away and I believe it sort of worked. I grew up reading Shakespeare, Conan Doyle, Ruskin Bond, Agatha Christie, Jane Austen, William Wordsworth, John Green, Lemony Snicket and many such marvelous writers and poets. Though one may not be able to create stories or write poems, one can always entertain themselves by reading the enriching literature that lets you explore the world, without having to move your feet.

7. ~mosaic

They say our dreams are our deepest desires and long-lost longings.

But what if these desires are being manifested in the unknown, With some spice and plot twists.

What if dreams are the fragments of our parallel universes?

Maybe that's why they make no sense at all…but still somehow do.

Dreams, dreams make you laugh, cry, fear and gasp. We travel to mystical lands and see monsters, gypsies and fairies and unbelievable creatures we haven't even known before. I personally think and it's a hypothesis that the things we see in our dreams, are nothing but incidences happening in the parallel universes around. Wouldn't it be fascinating? It definitely would. I do remember most of my dreams and that too crystal clear. It's crazy I know, but so am I ; so it's balanced. My dreams have always been this weird compilation of all the genres. Let me introduce you to some of my parallel universe incidences.

Enter Caption

1. Friend from the fair.
I stopped at the sight of the gravestone... It read,
R.I.P Ms. Lisa Thomas (2005-2018)
The wind roared and the wolves howled in distant land...

*My torch flickered, and off it went. It was all dark now.
I swallowed the bile rising up my throat, as I realised the reason
behind the weird glances of the crowd, when I was talking with
my new friend from the fair, Ms. Lisa Thomas....
I felt a sudden pain ran down my nerves, I felt weak, my legs
were heavy...
And then someone tapped from behind. The hand was cold and
the voice familiar. It was her, Lisa.
I gathered my guts,
I turned around and off went the light. I woke up gasping and
tried to catch my breath. I was sweating like a pig and my throat
went all dry. I was in my bed , "pffft, what a nightmare it was.",
I sighed. While going into the kitchen to quench my thirst, I
stumbled upon something and when I looked up I could not
believe what stood before my eyes. It was Lisa. Staring dead into
my eyes; "Hi there, dear friend.", she said in a raspy voice and
came onto me.
I screamed, so loud that I scared myself. It was a dream into
another dream. Boy , could it be anymore scary. I checked myself
if I was still dreaming. Fortunately I wasn't , because my 6:00
PM alarm started blaring; I had to get ready for the annual fair*

.

2. Nobody knows.

*It was a very hard time, we were at war. Me, Harry, Hermione,
Ron and the whole Hogwarts. At war with the one who's name
should not be taken. You know who. I will though because "Fear
of a name only increases fear of the thing itself." Voldemort with*

his wicked army , stood infront of us. We all were on the battlefield with our wands and brooms ; flying in the air , casting spells on each other. The sky was painted metallic and lighting bolted every ten seconds. We fought until we made the Dark Lord vulnerable and then I stepped forward and swished my wand. "Avada Kedavara!", I spelled out; and the light escaped my wand. It struck him and he collapsed. "Now you are a nobody knows!" (No body nose) , I exclaimed and death embraced him quick.

3. How to run away from your possessed wife - 101
I was a guy. Yes you heard me right. I was a guy in my dream this time and that too (drumroll) a married one. I was handsome looking and my wife, very elegant and beautiful; but was possessed. That is right, I was married guy with a good- lookng, possessed wife. Why not i mean. It is spooky, but make it pretty eh? She was all normal during the day but used to act all barbaric during the evenings.*
We had gathered in some basement for a exorcism, as it seemed when I took a look around. It was me, some unknown people and my wife. Suddenly she started crying hysterically and came to hug me. I knew something was fishy about the entire situation. So I pulled her away and to my surprise, she started turning into plastic. A plastic barbie. A possessed plastic barbie. It as a wicked sight, seeing her become this way, and attack the others around.
When I saw her coming for me, I started running away and all of a sudden the floor beneath me, began to rise and before I

know it, I was up in the air. Not very nice of me to leave my possessed wife behind like that eh? Well I did it anyway. And that is the origin story, of the book - How To Run Away From Your Possessed Wife - 101.

Well now that you've gotten a glimpse of my wicked dreams, you now know the power of imagination. Well not really one's imagination, but the way our brain works is just fascinating. Dreams are a boon. They let you escape from the cruel reality into a wonderland where sorrow is not known and darkness is nothing but a mere word. Nightmares on the other hand are scary but still thrilling. To sum it up, everything related to human mind, is exciting and mesmerizing. Your mind is a powerful weapon, use it wisely and don't let your demons take control.

8. ~the unsent unexpressed

The letters of my mind, which were never read to anyone, nor did I peeped in by myself again. The letters that were never really written, neither posted, nor shown. They remained unknown...
There are things that are often left unexpressed. The things that you wanted to tell, the people you wanted to bind. The statements that remain unstated, the words that weren't uttered at all.
The feelings that you hesitated to show, the emotions that you buried deep below. The questions you wanted to ask, the answers you wanted to give.
Tons to show and heaps to know. ALWAYS.

[If we could do things, the way we are supposed to do,
Then it would have been all perfect throughout our lives.
But it isn't for a reason...
And that is because, life is all about the little imperfections and flaws that sum up it's beauty; that makes us more of what we really are...
A human.]

Enter Caption

Now let me tell you a story.
Once upon a time, there was a little girl named Daisy. She was
smart and bubbly and full of life. When it came to expressing
her feelings though, she lacked a little, because she cared too
much about what others would think of her. That they might get
a wrong impression of her, misunderstand her, and that the
things would go downhill. Though she was just 10, she was very
thoughtful and considerate.
So, whenever she had anything to say, to her family or her
friends, which was hard for her to get off her chest; she use to
write letters to them. Never sent any though. The letters used to
be very specific and she would let go of her, through her words.

She felt safe within those paper spaces. Far from the fear of being misunderstood. The letters were her comfort zone.

On a summer Sunday, her beloved grandma Katherine came to visit her. After having a delicious cuisine, made by Daisy's mother, Daisy took her grandma upstairs to her room. They chatted a lot and grandma told her various stories about fairies, mystical lands, gypsies, angels, ogres, mermaids, of witches and warlocks, kings and queens, and all such fascinating creatures. Daisy was keenly listening to all of them with a twinkle of curiosity in her eyes. While Daisy was lost into the land of wonders, she was just introduced to, her grandma noticed something. A round box with a purple ribbon on the top, that was peeking out of the pile of her storybooks. She asked Daisy about the box. Daisy brought that box to her grandma and told her all about the letters. Grandma Katherine took her little granddaughter's hands in hers and said,

" My sweet little Daisy, you don't need to hide away your thoughts and feelings like this. I understand that it can be hard sometimes, to open up and it is good that you have found this beautiful way of doing so and that you care about those around you; but the thing is , though you write it out, these letters of yours, you keep them to yourself. Do you post them? No right? So people never really have a chance to understand you, to know you better. People who make you happy, sad or they hurt you or make you feel anything for that matter of fact; you need to tell them. Don't you think, most of the times they deserve to know? And more than them deserving to know it, you owe it to yourself

too. We are all humans, we are bound to make mistakes. People will hurt eachother, intentionally, unintentionally and we are bound to have different opinions about different things. You don't have to agree with all that they have to say to you, but what you can do is listen. Get to know this world a little better. That is how you will be able to form your own set of opinions about various things. That is how you will have a voice of your own.

The ones who love you and care for you, would listen to you. They would not judge you, for who you are. Those who do, are the ones we better stay off; but you won't know that if you don't put yourself out there. We all need to learn our lessons by our own and sometimes the hard way. Misunderstandings occur, you just have to talk it out. Afterall communication is the key right? So, from now onwards, speak yourself, speak your heart. Would you do that? Not for me or your parents, but for yourself?, she asked.

"Ay Ay Captain!", Daisy exclaimed. Her innocence made grandma chuckle.

She took the letters out of the box and rushed out of the room.

"Where are you off to?", grandma asked.

"To post them!", Daisy said with a grin.

" Okay, but won't you give your grandma a kiss first?", grandma said while catching Daisy downstairs and pulling her into a hug.

She kissed grandma Katherine and rushed outside.

{ You are sad, cry out an ocean.
You are happy, laugh out loud, grin left to right.
You are angry, break a dish or two.
You are excited, shout and squeal.
You are afraid, face your fear, stare dead into it's eyes.
You are in love, let the warm-fuzzy feeling indulge into you.
Be vulnerable, but don't let them step all over you.
Be kind, but also let them know your worth.
Take it slow, one step at a time..
And eventually, you'll be just fine. }

9. ~it's a good day to be here, it's a good day to be queer.

Love-is-Love

They crossed the lane together,

Hands entwined...

Unaware of the stares ,

The lovers gone blind....

Destined towards freedom,

They walked with pride...

The Rainbow in their hearts,

Glows fierce and bright...

Eternal they stand, for all who love,

For those who go beyond and for those who want to...

Giving a whole new meaning to love and to life,

Breaking all the walls, they vibrantly outshine...

Though parted by misfortune,

Vibgyor held them together...

Nutured by warmth, their love grows forever.

My favourite uncles, uncle Gabriel and uncle Patrick are the loveliest couple I've ever seen. They are happy-go-lucky and charming everytime I see them. That doesn't mean they don't have to go through difficulties in life , but they face them with a smile on their face and a hope in their hearts for everything to be alright someday. It wasn't easy for them to be a gay couple and wanting to adopt a child at their time. It's still not that easy, but I know it will be one day. However, things went well and they did adopt a girl child . Avery, was 6 months old when my uncles brought her home and ever since then, they have loved and nurtured her from the bottom of their heart. Avery is now 3 years old and she's a very smart and happy kid . She lits up every room she's in, with her baby talk and giggles. My uncles have came a long way and have gone through a lot, but they never gave up on eachother and their love. I feel very lucky for having them as my uncles , because they are the best. Whenever I want any life advice I go to mom and dad, yes; but I feel like my uncles are better at giving advice and overall understanding me. I feel like I can share anything and everything with them and they are soo good at keeping secrets. Not just all this, but also that they have created a safe space, not just for me but for anyone who needs to open up . I aspire to be a good person like them, as I proceed to growup.

• LGBTQ+ , the standard abbreviation is fairly straightforward, 'Lesbian, Gay, Bisexual and Transgender.' The 'Q' stands for 'questioning' or 'queer' ; for the ones who still are exploring their true self. Actually, there is no need to classify people under

different tags, but sadly they have to do so, sadly they have to go through, themselves being put into different boxes. All of this fuss because, we are incapable of understanding simple things and because we just make it complicated for ourselves and lack the basic knowledge. They are humans with emotions and not objects with labels. We are living in 21st century and we need to expand our thinking and change our perspectives for the good , towards the sunshine. But when it comes to accept people who are different from us, we always lack. They are just normal people , like you and me. With two hands, to legs and a face, who carry a rainbow in their hearts. They are unique and beautiful in their own way. Liking someone or being attracted to someone of the same gender, isn't disgusting or something to be ashamed of. Making fun of those who are different from us, we don't prove ourselves superior or them inferior. Instead we show how narrow minded and immature we are; we just become less of a human being and more of a monster. It is no rocket science to get this in your head. There is no need for the queer, to change. It is us, who need to be more accepting and open towards the world, to take a look from other's glasses too ; and to just imagine how it would be, to be in their shoes. Afterall, as they say and I quote "LOVE IS LOVE" and it isn't bounded in the limits of someone's gender. Everyone deserves to be happy and cherished by their significant one, because...

LOVE IS LOVE

"Everybody loves somebody sometime
Everybody falls in love somehow
Something in your kiss just told me
That sometime is now
Everybody finds somebody someplace
There's no telling where love may appear
Something in my heart keeps saying
My someplace is here..."
- Dean Martin & Deana Martin

10. ~knight in the shining armor

No one's gonna appreciate you,
Until you do. No one's gonna stand for you,
Until you do.

The alarm blared in my ears and I woke up to a very pleasant Monday morning. I say pleasant, because that day I was going to Aunt Adele's in the Pacifica, CA.

Aunt Adele and Victor got married very young, they struggled alot during the beginning but together, they managed to get out of it and bought their first home. A little lake house by the countryside of Pacifica, CA. A couple of years after that, they moved to San Diego.

Uncle Victor, passed away after their 25 years of togetherness. Aunt Adele lost the love of her life, she went into depression; and the first two weeks of therapy were very hard for her. As time passed by, she grew around the trauma. She grew mentally, by each passing day. She was a strong-willed woman and learnt to cherish the moments that she had spent with her lovely husband.

"Sometimes, it is not necessary that your journey will end the way you want it to.
So you just have to learn from the adventures and save the polaroids."

❦❦❦

She moved back to the countryside lake house where her heart resided. It's been awhile now, and since it were my vacations, I decided to visit her. Aunt Adele is a person, who is always very vibrant. She is fun and outgoing and I love to be around her. It's like there are some people in this world, whose presence itself makes it easier for us.
I finally reached my aunt's place and was amazed by the natural beauty of it . It was a cosy warm place in the amidst of the mountains and a magnificent lake. I was in love with the place , and I was going to have a blast. That night aunt and I made pizza together and danced all night to the "MAP OF THE SOUL" album. Aunt Adele is a 20 year old trapped inside a 45 year old's body.
The next day I woke up to a beautiful scenario outside the window of my room. The lake water was sparkling under the bright sun and the birds were singing songs of happiness. Aunt made my favourite Belgium waffles for breakfast and asked me if I wanted to go to wallmart with her later. I said no because I wanted to enjoy the solitude and paint for awhile. My aunt left the house by 4PM after lunch and I, after taking a quick nap sat down for painting, on my little canvases.

After finishing my painting, I got up to see if aunt had any softdrinks in the refrigerator. I was about to enter the kitchen, that's when I saw a blurred figure outside. Aunt had warned me of the wildlife, but it wasn't some animal. Then I heard some movement outside the house and thus I slowly but steadily approached the windows. I saw a full grown man with a weird mask on , trying to peek into the house. I quickly ducked down and a chill went down my spine. "Is this guy trying to break in?", "He must have a weapon, oh my god what do I do now?" "My cell's in my room and if I walk in there the guy could see me " all kinds of thoughts crept into my mind. That's when I heard the door creak and open. The guy had broken into the house. I couldn't let him know that I was there, because that would be me risking my own life . I had to do something, I wasn't just going to let him rob my aunt like that. I had to think of a plan and not do anything stupid. I hid below the kitchen counters, as the guy went in one of the bedrooms. As he fully went into the room , I slowly got up and without making any noise, grabbed the knife off the platform. He came outside and was coming towards the kitchen. My heart paced faster as I heard the footsteps that came closer. That's when the telephone rang; must have been my aunt. The guy quickly turned around and without thinking for a second or two I got up and threw the knife at him . He got stabbed by it, into his lower back and he led out a scream out of pain. His eyes pierced my soul as he looked at me and slowly removed the knife. I ran into my room as he came after me and closed the door behind me and locked it. I put the

*dressing table infront of it, to the hold the door for a little longer.
He started banging loudly and even shot a bullet or two through
it. I saw my cell on the bed and called 911 and my aunt. She
was super panicked and was on the way. I wanted someone so
bad to come and rescue me , as I stood there like a drenched deer,
in vincinity of a cruel huntsman. That's when I saw my aunt's
shotgun on the wall . She used to tell me the stories of her and
uncle Victor going on for hunting and so I knew that she kept
bullets in the third drawer besides the bed in every room. I
gulped down my fear and took the shotgun and put some bullets
in it. I saw a catapult beside the pack of bullets and some stones.
I was good with catapults, but I had never held a shotgun in my
entire life; I mean 17years of my existence on this planet. The
guy was seconds away from breaking the door. I hid behind the
big cupboard as he barged into the room and took a look
around. He bent down to look beneath the bed . He was about
to get up , I stretched my catapult with all my strength and hit
his hand; making him loose his gun. I hit his forehand too,
which made him whine even more. I started shooting the
shotgun in the air , which made him duck down and then
somehow I managed to shoot him in his leg after breaking three
of the frames on the wall. Sirens were wailing outside until then
and I opened the window and jumped outside. I ran towards my
aunt and she hugged me tightly. The police got the thief and
went after doing some questioning and some more investigation.
Me and my aunt both cried for sometime, for she was terrified
and I was bombarded with all sorts of emotions. She said she*

was very proud of me for the way I handled everything bravely. I was proud of myself too. I was proud too, for all this time I thought someone else might come save me from this dreadful day, but turns out that I was my own knight in the shining armor.

Not just in situations like this but in everyday life too. You have to remember one thing that you have to stand-up for yourself first. People can help you, advice you in certain situations or guide you towards light but it's you who has to take your own decisions. That is because you and only you have seen yourself closely, going through the thick and thin; you know your weaknesses and you know your inner strength. You know what you are capable of and that is everything. You are capable of doing anything and everything if you make up your mind, never believe anything else.

VOLUME 002

THE FOLK - TALES

11. ~bubbles

I was gazing out of the car window, it was raining heavily and Earth's pleasant scent was all in the air. There was a toad out in the front, chasing a tiny, blue butterfly. The butterfly was teasing him , oh but it looked like he was having a great time. Good for him!

Kai dropped me home and kissed me goodbye.

I had just got out of the shower. Made a hot cocoa for myself and snuggled up in a blanket with "The Fault In Our Stars". I was reading the part where Hazel reads the letter to Augustus. It was so beautifully written. It reminded me of the time when someone special had written a crazy letter for me, couple of years ago .

Bubbles.

Enter Caption

Bubbles was no ordinary guy, there was something very special about him, about his whole aura. I was 14 when I met bubbles. I was looking for new books in a store down the street, because you just can not get enough. Am I right or am I right? Well, I was looking for something in the horror/thriller section. Stefen King's "The Stand" caught my eyes I went to get the book off the rack, but somehow I couldn't. It was being pulled from the other side too. I pulled it hard and saw this cute angry face through the gap, that was formed. "Better luck next time", I said as I rolled my eyes at him. I went into the next aisle to look for another book to make the purchase and after that went to a small cafe in the area to read in peace.

"Is this seat taken?", he asked.

"No ..you?" I recognised him from the library. It was bubbles the angry chihuahua.

"Are you following me?" , I asked.

"Are you serious? No. Of course not. May I sit now?". I nodded yes and we got talking.

He was really a very interesting human. He was tall, had black curly hair with silver highlights which looked surprisingly good on him and also complimented his blue ocean-like eyes. Athletic body with a great sense of fashion plus humour and fondness for good books, oh my my, he was one heck of a guy. He looked adorable when he was angry. Everytime we used to talk , it was me ranting about stuff and he listening to it with a curious face.

He adored my weirdness and I, his . With him it wasn't just conversations, he was so thoughtful and considerate about things and had strong opinions and a very unique way to look at the world and things going around...it was actually very impressive. We used to meet on the weekends and hangout at the cafe talking about random stuff and sometimes, doing nothing together. He was becoming a habit of mine and I knew that I liked him very much.

Once while in the cafe he asked me, "would you like to have coffee with me?"

"Wait, isn't that we what we do here on a regular basis?", I laughed. I was just so silly. Still am, nothing's really changed.

"No, like would you like to go on a date with me?" , he asked with a shy smile.

I could sense the nervousness in his voice. Oh he was so shy and cute and I wanted this to happen from so long. "Well, I thought you'd never ask.", I said giving him a soft smile.

It was my first ever date. Bubbles took me to a book-cafe in the town because a bookstore was where we first met and he wanted it to be a little nostalgic. He loved planning such things and he was so good at it. We went on a couple of dates after that and later we started hanging out at eachother's places. Mom and dad liked him too ...well how can someone not like bubbles I mean. He was such a sweetheart. He loved doing karaoke evenings and used to sing at the top of his lungs when it was any metal genre song. He looked like a hyped up chihuahua while vibing with his favourite songs. He even let me paint his nails! I loved how he didn't hesitate to break the stereotypes and always stood by my side. It was only a matter of time for me to fall for him, and I did. Oh I fell so hard. I knew he liked me . He used to take me out for bicycle rides and then we used to sit by the lake, our feet dipped into water. He knew I was all for old school romances, so he wrote me a letter. Of course he did.

12. ~the letter - 1

Dear Audrea,

I sit to write a letter to you, and I am all five again; there's a lot to say to you but somehow I don't know how to form proper sentences!wow. There is just something about you, that makes me loose my mind(in a good way:)) and I just go blank ,the way I used to before the exams, but so much better. I scribble and scribble and then tear the page off, crumble it. I wanted this to be so perfect, but I know better now. It isn't supposed to be perfect, it's just supposed to be from the bottom of my heart. The first time I saw you, my heart skipped a beat and I just knew that you were gonna become this important part of my life. I want you to know that, my atoms have always loved your atoms, ever since they have know you. Infact, they have never stopped loving your atoms. Well I don't know what I am talking anymore haha..or how much this makes sense to you; but I know this for sure that ever since I have laid my eyes on you, there hasn't been a day where I haven't thought about you. You live in my mind 24/7 rent-free. And sometimes I wonder..I wonder if you think about me frequently or do you even think about me? Do you think about me? Do you think about me the way I do? I am someone who has super commitment issues; but something about you takes my fear away and makes me want to be with you till forever and ever. As if you take my hands in yours, running your fingers through my curls , you whisper in my ear, "everything will be alright, we will be alright; because you and me, we belong together. Never believe anything else." A single 'hey' from you is enough to make my the organs in my body go crazy. Whenever you compliment me or as a matter of fact anything and everything that you say to me, runs on my mind the whole day , making me smile goofily like an idiot. You make my heart bloom and my day merrier.

Though you are not around always, I can breathe you in the air. Always in an awe of how well you know me in so less time and the way you just get me without having to say anything. With you by my side, I can never be miserable. "It is rare to find someone so effortlessly adorable like you, when you are around my sky is always blue. The way we talk, things you say, the way you make it all okay. And how you know all of my jokes but you laugh anyway. If I could wish for a thing, I'd take the smile that you bring; wherever you go in this world I'll come along." Yes, I know, I know, it's the barbie song that we always sing along.

I just want to be somebody to you. Somebody to whom you return when you are happy or you are blue. Somebody who will hold your hand and be by your side, somebody to watch the starry night sky with , leaving all your worries aside. As Hazel says, "some infinities are bigger than the other infinities; and I'm very grateful for our little infinity here." I have been holding back , holding back myself from feeling anything real , because I don't want to get hurt and I don't want to go through all that pain again. But being with you, I tend to think differently. I have realised that with love there is loss, that's the part of the deal. Sometimes it hurts, but in the end, everything is worth it. You are worth it. Worth all of it. I want to give you my heart and soul.

It is only with the heart that one can see rightly; what is essential is invisible to the eye. And from what I know,...

13. ~the letter - 2

*Love is being willing to ruin a good painting for a chance at a greater one; and love is messy and horrible and selfish and bold. It makes you do crazy things, but oh they feel so good. Love makes your life a bit less hard and a little bit more bearable. Love gives you wings(not like red bull. Lol *why am I like this:))to soar high across the widespread blue. Love makes you blush until the last shade of red makes you feel lighter than a feather and happier that the daffodils along the bay, basking in the warm sun.*

So now, now I set my heart free to wonder in the garden of love and ponder around your familiar scent. You and me , we are the Dandelions. Wild and free and can't be bought by anyone. I let my heart breathe in the sweet air and let the fiery feeling indulge into me. For now I know from the pit of my stomach and the deep centre of my bones, from the crown of my skull and from the bottom of my heart that resides in my hollow chest, that, that..I Love You!

I love you to all the infinite summersaults my heart did whenever I saw you, talked to you or even thought about you..and back. You have clouded my thoughts and I'm loving it. You have started growing on me and I hope I am growing onto you too. There are billions of people on this planet but none of them is you. I have never wrote a letter like this to anyone, but here I am ranting my heart out to you. Don't mind me if I go off track or just blabber about stuff. Well because you know by now, that I do that a lot. Nervous ranting.

I get scared sometimes, not denying it, because.. because love is scary too. It's scarier than you want to admit it is; but it's not like in the movies. It is better, because it is real. Lara Jean said it herself. Plenty of people are good-looking, but that doesn't make then interesting or intriguing or cool. You my dear are my happy place. You are all that I ever looked for . My perfect is you and I can be the realest version of myself around you. I ardently admire you and would savour your weirdest quirks; because love is worth everything, everything. Isn't it? I have been in love before, but this time with you, it feels so real, I feel so alive like never before. Falling in love with you , I fall in love with myself too. I didn't know that was possible.

I don't remember not knowing you. It feels like, you and me we go way back. There is this connection between us, this energy that we share; you make me believe in us, in magic. I can float into your dreamy eyes for as long as I am alive ; you is where my heart resides. We'd be skin on skin and yet I would pull you closer. I want to be kissing you rather than missing you. Lets spread our wings together and reach the skies, take different shapes alongside the clouds where the solitude lies. And we'll meet each other at the horizon of love, where the earth reunites with the sky.

You dear Audrea are my lobster! I want to be with you on Monday, Tuesday, till the very sunday of the week. Into your arms is where I find my peace. Your smile, oh your smile lightens up my entire life and your laughter is like a remedy to my once wounded heart. How do I tell you how much you mean to me? Any statement for that matter of fact would be an understatement. I will never stop loving you, even though you turn into a little chipmunk one day, I would carry you in my pocket wherever I go . Always. I am ready to take all the efforts, but would you meet me the halfway?

{I want your sweet caress

I dream of your tenderness

Oh I never, ever felt like this

I swear

Look what you've done to me

Oh boy, it's poetry

When I see the wind in your hair

The tears well up inside

Oh, what will turn the tide

And I've been waiting for you to decide

That you love me too

Since I laid eyes on you

- Faith Hill}

All I want to say is that if I am a fool for falling in love with you, then so shall I be. There has not been anything that I've longed for so much, the way I long for being with you.

~ by the hand of his , who would willingly remain yours ♡

Enter Caption

• *A tear glided onto my cheeks as I slowly folded the letter. It felt like I have unboxed the memories of my past. When I read this letter for the first time , I knew I would want to read it until forever. I was left speechless, I somehow always knew I fell for the right person. Bubbles and I were together for a long time, but he shifted far away and unfortunately we couldn't make it work. [It is sad when two people love eachother a lot but cannot make it work.]*

You will always have a soft spot for the person you loved once..and that is completely normal. You can not forget someone you once were immensely in love with. It is impossible to do so.

14. ~ladybird

Enter Caption

"Oh, look! what a pretty bird! Do you know what it's called?",
Amy asked .
Her big brown eyes were twinkling with wonder.

"Oh yes, it's an Eastern bluebird.", I replied.

"Whoa, it looks so beautiful. It would be so much fun , if I could fly like the birds.", she said admiring the bird flying gracefully across the widespread blue.

"Yeah it would be pretty awesome. We would be able to see the entire world from up there and go wherever we want, whenever we want.", I said.

"That's exactly what my grandma says. You know she says that she bets the world looks like a mystical land from up there and that birds they always fly together as a flock, though they are individually exploring. The unity that they showcase and the way they protect eachother is really inspiring.", she said playing with a twig .

❧❧❧

Amy was indeed a very bright and lively little girl. I met her while on a road trip to a Lake near the countryside. It was spring break, so my friends and I had decided to go on a little trip. We had booked a cottage near the lake area and we were going to enjoy a little solitude. When we reached there we all were in love with the place and the entire surrounding. There were fields and meadows, farm animals and orchards around the place.

The scenery was so serene, as if it was painted by Van Gogh. Carnival of scents blew in the air and a horde of dandelions littered the meadow. Versace-purple crocuses seemed to glow before our eyes. Jewel-green grasshoppers bounced atop the grass like leggy trampolines. In the stony verges, Rafael-red valerian sprouted from between coral-black cracks. Spears of dawn light suddenly drenched the farthest corners with their golden magic. I walked towards the lake. The water was glistening under the sun and the breeze was gently caressing my cheeks. I saw someone sitting by the lake. It was a little girl, in a cute yellow frock and had her hair braided with red ribbons.

"May I sit here?", I asked. She looked at me and nodded yes. Her eyes were dark brown, the kind of brown that shines like amber crystals in bright sunlight ; cheeks were rosy red and she smiled so softly, oh it melted my heart.

"Hii! My name is Audrea.", I shook her hand.

"I am Amy, I live nearby."

"Do you come here often?", I asked.

"Yes, I like the lake very very much , this much!", she said widening her arms.

"Aw!", I grinned.

"Are those your friends over there?", Amy asked.

"Yes, we came here on a trip. They were deciding to go to a escape room or something and trying to get everyone aboard. But I stopped listening when they opened there mouth.", I said and Amy giggled.

She had some cupcakes with her and offered me one. "Do you like mint flavoured cupcakes?", she asked. "Like it , I love it!", I exclaimed.

"I love them too! Heeh", she smiled goofily. "You know, I have a little sister Hailey, she is 5 years old and she loves cupcakes so

much and especially with chocochips on the top. And mom, mom loves to bake for us. She makes us delicious meals everyday and on weekends mom and dad cook together.", she said.

"That's so cute . Your family seems so adorable..just like you.", I booped on her nose.

"What does your dad do?", I asked.

"Oh he is a carpenter. He makes really good furniture and also plays with me and hailey whenever he is home. On weekends, in the evening we all go to the park and have lots of fun and icecream!", she exclaimed.

I sat there for almost an hour, talking with her and listening to all the interesting things she had to share. She loved reading books , the way she was talked so passionately about different books that she read and telling me all the stories, I was in an awe. Me and my friends stayed at the cottage for about a week and everyday I used to meet Amy by the lake in the mornings . She use to bring me flowers and I gave her my books to read until I was there. (I always carry books with me, no matter what) She fell in love with Ruskin Bond's " The Blue Umbrella" and "Matilda".

It was our last day at the lake . I went to the lake in the morning but Amy wasn't there. After I finished packing , I decided to visit Amy's and give her the books. I asked around for where she lives . I reached her house and knocked on the door. An old lady opened the door . She smelled like fresh baked cookies and looked so fragile and tiny yet very motherly.

"May I help you with anything dear?", she asked me.

" You must be her grandma. Amy's grandma. I am Audrea , I wanted to meet Amy. ", I said.

" Oh Audrea! Amy talks about you so much, she really admires you. You are a very sweet girl. Come on in. ", she said with a smile and led me inside her house.

"Thankyou grandma. Is Amy here?", I asked.

"Oh I'm sorry dear Amy has a little cold from yesterday so she's sleeping. ", her grandma said.

"Oh okay. I hope she gets well soon. ", I said. "By the way, where are her parents and umm, hailey her sister. I would love to meet them too. I brought these cupcakes with extra chocochips on the top for Hailey, and these books are for Amy. "

Her grandma looked at me oddly, as if she was trying to figure out something. Her voice broke a little and she said,

"Oh that's so sweet of you my dear, but Amy doesn't has a little sister. Amy's parents. ", her grandma handed me a photoframe. "They died in an accident when Amy was just a baby. Since then it's just me and Amy. ", her grandma said , her smile faded away.

"Oh I am so sorry for your loss. I had no idea. Amy told me these things. I am so sorry. Oh poor Amy, how she must have handled all this. ", I said shocked.

"Amy is a very strong girl you see. She helps me a lot around and god bless her soul for she is my only family and I hers. I call her my moonpie. She must've told you that. She reads these books, the stories within them and has her own world of imagination where she paints a picture of how it would have been if her parents were alive. Then she talks so passionately and her eyes do *this happy dance. She goes to the lake every morning, everyday, because once she had a dream where she saw her parents sitting on a bench by that lake and now she hopes that maybe one day she will meet them there.", her grandma said with watery eyes. "I don't know what to say. I feel heartbroken knowing that such a good little kid like her is devoid of a family. I am glad she has such a loving grandma like you though, to be there to take care of her and to be there for her."*

I gave the books and the cupcakes to her grandma and told her to tell Amy that she is a very bright girl and the sweetest one I have ever come across. I left the house and me and my friends got on the road, back home. Don't know about the others, but I was returning home with a heavy heart and lots of good memories by the lake.

15. ~Ms. Valerie

She looked in the mirror...
There was dark beneath her eyes
But all she could see, was the hardwork that made her thrive.
Wrinkles by her side, didn't bother her at all,
For all she remembered was the smiles she'd been blessed with.
Her poor sight never stood in her way..since she was
accompanied by her souvenirs
The intricate articles, the daisies and the familiar scent.
Grey in her hair , was from the journey that was worth for...
She was growing old, she was becoming the very pure essence.

Ms. Valerie had just moved next-door. She was old, but didn't like being called grandma. The children on the block learnt it the hard way; but otherwise she was a very lovely person, though it seemed a little hard to believe. She was one of those people, who seemed to be rude and mean from the outside but once you spend time with them, there isn't a soul more genuine.
Ms. Valerie had a beautiful front yard. Lush green grass all over , lined with red, yellow, white and pink coloured shrubs of roses. She took good care of all her plants. Had Bougainville hanging infront of her front door and a big orange tree with different

varieties of shrubs in the backyard. Turns out, Ms. Valerie was a biologist and had recently retired, thus decided to move here in San Francisco. She also had a very adorable little fellow, his name was coco. He was a Labrador. It had been only a couple of weeks for them moving into the house next door, but since the time I played catch with him, he was just always there for me.

Mom invited Ms. Valerie over for dinner once.

Ms. Valerie brought us a cute little cactus plant . She was one of a kind I must say. The dinner went good and we got to know our neighbour a little better. I used to go to her house frequently. We used to chat about different things. Life, studies, boys and a lot of stuff. She used to show me her collection of various plants and flowers. She had a separate room for that. To be honest, she was too cool for anyone. Not everyone got her, but those who did, loved her a lot. From the little kids to the parents of the little kids, everyone admired her.

She used to help me convince my parents for parties and many a times help me sneak out too. At the same time , made me make things right whenever I screwed up. She was cool but not reckless, she was sweet and also sassy, she had a balance in life. I got to learn a lot from her.

One fine day, while chilling with my friends at my house I heard Ms. Valerie call my name. We went over at hers and saw her on the floor. Apparently, she had fallen down from a big stool, in order to get something down and then she twisted her ankle and couldn't get up. We helped her get up and got her some water.

"What were you trying to do? You could have got hurt much bad
you know!", I said.
"Well I had to get that box from up there.", she said.
"What the rush? I could have helped you.", I said.
"I know, but I didn't want to bother you guys . You do so much
for me already. ", she said making me sit beside her.
"Oh common , you don't bother us. Plus we love hanging out
with you and coco. He makes my day even better and happier.
So , anyways what were you looking for in that box?", I asked.
I got on the stool and brought the box down. There were tons of
letters and pictures inside.
Looked vintage.

1.Dear Val,
Just like my morning coffee,
You give me a fresh start.
Just like a stuck up song,
You keep going on in my mind.
Just like my canvas,
You inspire me to experiment.
Just like my crazy will,
You excite me to break my shell.
Just like another story,
To tempt me till the end.
You are an adventure,
Much to explore and much more to discover...

The one which you want to never get over.
It's you who make my life better
Everyday Everyday.
Forever yours,
Meg

2. Dear Val,
Dressed as a night sky,
She gave hope to my dreary nights.
Carved from amber,
She held stars in her eyes.
She was the beautiful sunrise,
With the blend of orange and red.
Carrying spring in her curls,
She blossomed the way ahead.
Forever yours,
Meg

3. Dear Val,
Standing at the beach, listening to the waves, together as we
watch the sunset,
You hold my hand and the world stood still.
My heart stirred a bit and so did yours
I whispered in your ear tucking back the strand of your wavy
hair ,

Fondling your cheeks, I said,
"I'll always love you one scoop more."
Forever yours,
Meg

4. Dear Val,
You are the only reason I wake up in the morning. It's you who
makes me want to be a better version of myself. It's you who
taught me that it's okay, to not be okay and pushed me a little
harder towards self love.
In this mundane routine of life , meeting you is what I await the
most. You are my happy place. My pavilion. I love you to all the
infinities and back.
Forever yours,
Meg

5. Dear Val,
Look at me , tell me what you see...deep blue ocean or the sky
caught in stills?
Look at me , tell me what you see...my breathing soul or the
places I want to be?
The twinkle in my eyes, seeks for a tranquil gaze. My throbbing
heart, wants a safe escape.
Wind gushes through my hair, the sunlight strokes my cheeks. I
feel so alive, oh I feel so free..

Dancing in the moonlight , now you hold me close, your breath tickles my senses ..it tickles my toes.

All laughter fills the air, our faces lit up with impish glee... I want this to never end, for we are all just stardust. You and me.

Forever yours,

Meg

The box had all these beautiful love letters. All these archaic pages and everlasting love just overflowing out of them. When asked, Valerie said, " These were from my girlfriend Margot. I used to call her Meg. We met at this really antique museum and got talking. We shared the same interests and until Margot , I didn't really knew that I was interested in girls too. She wasn't just my girlfriend but before that she was my best friend. Something about her just seemed right , she used to get me like no one else could. Her eyes used to sparkle when she used to get excited about things. We used to write eachother letters. Though we met frequently, we kept writing to eachother because it felt like our love was being woven through our words. Her parents found about us and they restricted her from seeing me ever again. We tried alot, she tried a lot to make her parents understand us; but they did not listen at all. They took her away and our them seemingly possible lovestory, became just 'used to be's. Although there has never been a single day where I haven't thought about her or the way she smiled and the way she looked at me. I got a habit of her, and I am afraid, that one day I might not be able to remember her face, the color of her eyes, her hair, her glistening skin.", tears rolled down her cheeks and she told us to go home, for she needed to be alone.

I felt bad for Ms. Valerie. I made up my mind. I decided to find out if Margot was still alive or where she was. Luckily I did find her.

I wrote to her about Ms. Valerie on E- mail and to my surprise, she replied in a day. She missed Ms. Valerie too, but had no idea where she was. After me sending her the address, she came to visit Ms. Valerie.

Turns out neither Valerie nor Margot married anyone else. Both of them never stopped loving eachother. Eventually they started going out and got along again and decided to get married! It was the most beautiful and lovely ceremony I have ever attended in my entire life. Both of them were looking absolutely gorgeous and happy.

After putting the ring on Ms. Margot's finger, Ms. Valerie turned to me and said, "you know what they say right? ... Always marry your bestfriend!" and gave me a wink.

Enter Caption

16. ~the ghost of Arthur Willow - 1

"Once upon a time, in the village of Szar lived a man named Arthur Willow. He was tall , well built and had jet-black eyes. He was a very kind man and had never hurted a single soul. All the villagers were very fond of him and his whole aura. He was a lumberjack. He had a beautiful wife and two lovely children. One day while chopping the wood in the forest , suddenly the weather got cloudy and strong winds started to blow. It was as if the monsoons were near. He decided to hurry up and head home before it got dark and dangerous. On his way home he heard someone weeping by the river.

It was getting dark but he couldn't leave that person alone in the forest. He went in the direction of the sound and saw a little kid sitting on a log beside the river and he was crying. He went forward to ask the kid but suddenly the kid ran towards the river and jumped into it. Arthur's eyes couldn't believe what he saw. He immediately put his bundle of logs down and ran towards the river . He couldn't see anyone in the water. Being confused and a little afraid he turned around and to his shock , there stood that little kid right behind him. Arthur took a step back and before he could say anything his leg slipped and he fell into the river. The flow of the river was really strong. Arthur cried for help but the kid just stood there staring at him blankly. Arthur couldn't make it and he got drowned away.

After hearing the news of her husband's tragic demise, Arthur's wife , Susanne became more than miserable. No one knew what exactly happened to him at the river. The whole village was in grief. Eventually, after a couple of weeks everyone went back to their daily routines and resumed their lives. Susanne though, could not get over the fact that her husband had passed away. Every single day was agony, she had sleepless nights and gloomy days. She wanted to meet him for one last time, she became really desperate. That night Susanne decided to summon Arthur's soul .", Uncle Cameron took a long pause and stopped.

I remember it was the Christmas holidays. All my relatives and cousins had come to our house for the Thanksgiving dinner. One of my uncles, uncle Cameron was very fond of telling horror stories to us. I was seven and my cousins a year or two younger and older. Me, Julie, Michelle, Sammy and Hailey had sat around on the rug in our PJ's listening to uncle Cameron's stories. He used to tell them with such dedication; raspy and spooky voice and all the required background noises; we all believed in his stories.

"Whoa..what happened next??", Sammy asked out of sheer curiosity.

"Well, Susanne summoned her husband and..", uncle continued.."and it all went downhill. The Arthur that made a contact with Susanne wasn't actually her husband. Technically

yes, but spiritually he wasn't the same loving and kind guy. The person that returned , ", he looked at all of us with wide eyes and said, "was vicious , it was a bad spirit. Susanne had led open a path into the living realm for a vicious spirit, an evil entity. Once died, upon summoning it is not necessary that the spirit that returns from another realm is a good one; because it creates an unbalance between the realms. The vicious spirit of Arthur started taking down the villagers one by one, creating a havoc."

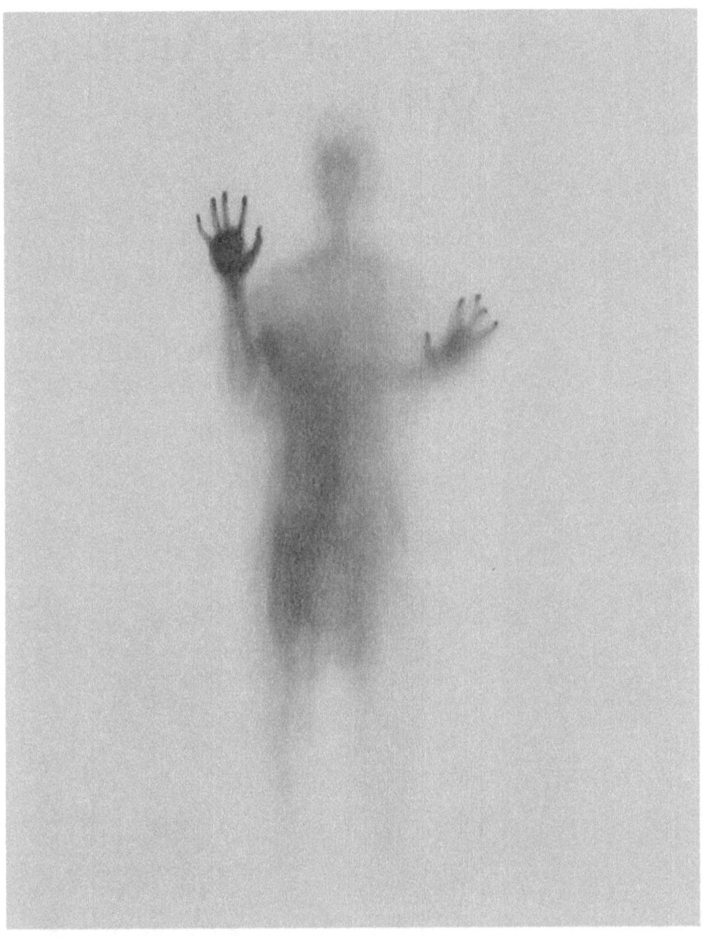

Enter Caption

17. ~the ghost of Arthur Willow - 2

Enter Caption

Susanne had led open a door to the unholy but was completely unaware of it. She was happy that she contacted to her dead husband and bid adieu. But did she really?", asked uncle.
We all stared at him, mouth wide open and at the edge of our imaginary seats.
"This is what happened next.", and he continued.
"1. What time is it?
Paul was coming home after a very long time, after almost a year. He was a fabric seller and used to go to the city frequently. He got offered a really good price by a fellow merchant and thus bought a shop in the city . Since then he used to come to the village once every year or two. In the village lived his old mother and father.
It was almost midnight when he was crossing the bridge. The moon was shining bright and there was nothing but solitude all around. Suddenly he heard a distant howl and barking of dogs, but there seemed no dogs around him . He got a little alarmed, fastening his pace ; now he was half a kilometre away from his house. He felt someone was walking very close behind him.
"Who would be it? That too at this ungodly hour. I don't know anyone else working so late in this village.", he thought to himself. "What time is it?", the man walking behind Paul asked.
Paul turned behind.
"Oh Arthur!", Paul smiled, he got a little relieved. "How have you been?", he asked.

Arthur said nothing but ,"what time is it?".
Paul found that a little weird but told him the time anyway, "It's
3:00AM."
They started walking again. Arthur kept walking behind Paul.
He asked him again, "what's the time?" Paul told him that it
was 3:05 AM. After sometime, Arthur asked him again, "what's
the time?" Paul got a little annoyed and turned around and
looked angrily at Arthur and then down at his watch. Paul
couldn't believe his eyes. Arthur's feet were a little above the
ground and backwards. A chill went down his spine and he
looked up in fear. Arthur's eyes were piercing into Paul's eyes.
Paul turned around and started running for his life. He ran and
ran until he found a nearby shed to take shelter. He was panting
heavily. After sometime, Paul peeked outside, to see if Arthur was
still out there. He wasn't.
Paul led out an exhilarating sigh and started walking towards
his house. "What's the time?", Arthur's voice came from behind
him. Paul's eyes became wide open and his legs froze. He wanted
to run but it felt as if he was glued to the ground. A minute
passed, he was just standing there , shaking. He tried to run and
he did . He ran so fast he directly crashed into his house. He tried
to speak but his mouth was all dry and he was sweating
tremendously. His body was burning up like fire and he fainted.
2. Many years had been passed now. The village got very well
developed and almost became a fully functioning little town of
Szar, with a central mall and cafes around the corner. Penny,
was driving out of the town , when she gave a lift to a man

standing halfway on the bridge. They started talking and he said that he was Arthur Willow a lumberjack. Penny had no idea who he was and thus kept talking to him. Half an hour passed and they could hear scratching noises coming from the car. Arthur told her to get down and check what was the issue; but she denied saying that, "the mechanic is not far away. We will get the car checked there." The noise kept coming and Arthur kept insisting her but she didn't get off. Eventually he got off the car and said goodbye to her. When she looked back from the car she saw no one behind her . It was as if Arthur vanished in thin air. Poof!

•"Why was he fixating so much on Penny to get down?", I asked my uncle. "Because...if she had got down the car, she would have been dead. Arthur the ghost would've killed her. ", he said in a very hoarse and spooky voice. Me and my cousins sat there around our uncle in pin drop silence being fascinated by the story and obviously a little afraid. (Okay a lot afraid) "tell us more!", Michelle said. "I will , I will. But first meet my friend...", Uncle Cameron pointed towards the door. It was a tall slender but very convincingly real doll of a man . It smelled funny and was looking very gruesome. "Arthur Willow!", He exclaimed and the doll popped up right infront of us. "Aaaaaahhhhhhhh!!!!!!", We all started screaming like maniacs and Sammy almost fainted. Uncle Cameron was laughing so hard that he fell off his chair and then we joined him too!

18. ~queens

Enter Caption

From a house wife, who works 24/7 without getting paid or any leave; happily taking care of her loved ones. Nurturing them with all the good and values ; giving out all that she has to satisfy their needs and to see them smile.

To a working woman, keeping her pace with time. Juggling her life, family and work. Managing all at once, not leaving any stone unturned. Tackling all the obstacles in order to maintain a balance..

They all are the Queens.

From a schoolgirl, figuring out her adolescence. Paving out a way through all the changes that she's going through both physically and mentally; and dealing with the daily challenges of responsibilities and emotions.

To a little flower girl by the roadside, 13 going on 30 . She has to earn a living at an age so small. Instead of books in her hand she has cuts and burns on her fragile palms; from having to feed her younger siblings. Learning the life lessons prior than needed, she still stands strong.

They all are the Queens.

From a sex worker , having to give her all in order to get the bare minimum and survive until she could. Wanting nothing but respect and understanding ; gulping down the helplessness and fighting all the hideous stares; wiping off her tears ...she thrives in a hope of a different sunrise.

To a business woman, building her own empire; sacrificing a lot in the process to make it upto the top , so she could make it a lot easier for the others willing to climb. Standing up on her own feet, being an equal and earning the well deserved respect and prosperity in this stand-offish and patriarchal society.

They all are the Queens.

From a Grandmother, been through life's crests and troughs. The white in her hair resembles her knowledge and wit. Having to please all those around, she knows better now. So she supports her women of the further generations, to be whatever they want to be ; for she sees herself in them here and there, bit by bit.
To a single girl, new in the city of dreams . All passionate with lots of dreams in her eyes, which twinkle with amaze as they gaze at the widespread shimmering concrete, all around. Striving to make her own identity and to make a difference. Not letting the society hold her back; she struts her way through. Holding her head up high.

They all are the Queens.

Fighting life's battles, now on their own terms,
Fiercely smashing the patriarchy.
Yes they bleed many a times, of pain and of betrayal, of sorrow and disappointment..
But they never give up .
Each time they've been pushed down to the rock bottom,
They've risen up high ,for sky is the limit.
Even more powerful and vibrant than before..
Their power comes from within and their hearts made of pure gold.

Standing up for each other, lending hands for the needy; together they soar across the blue.
Together they ROAR.

They are the reason of their own success, for they are the Queens of all Times.

A woman is a blend of love, warmth, talent, passion, motherhood, beauty, fierceness, strength, power, wisdom and the ability to achieve all of it once she makes up her mind. She is the Queen of all hearts. We have to keep supporting and inspiring those who aspire to make a difference. Even standing up against the wrong counts; and before standing up for others you need to learn to stand up for yourself.

One such very brave girl I know is Samantha Hudgens (Sam). Sam and I met during the summer camp of 2018 the "Birds of Paradise" She was tall with hair dyed blue and pink . Sam and I shared a cabin and every moment that I got to know her, I liked her even better. We shared a lot of stuff with eachother. One of the many things that Sam told me, this one hit me really hard and I learnt a lot out of it . I learnt a lot from her. Here it goes..

19. ~the mourning myrtle

It was good, until it wasn't.

> Until all that shimmered, was no good as gold.
> The wait was exhausting yet exhilarating, in the beginning.
> It felt worth it, worth all my patience,
> The efforts I made, the thoughts I put.
> We were so young, so full of compassion... so bold.
> That we took a leap of faith I believe, or so it's told.

It felt right, until it didn't.

> Until I felt nothing but suffocated, in your arms.
> You made me wait a little too longer...
> Our harmless chase, now became a dreadful race.
> You really thought you won? Aw, That's so sweet.
> I made you believe that you did.
> You really thought I was that easy to beat?

It was beautiful, until it wasn't

> Until your then seemingly breathtaking eyes,

Now made my skin crawl and vanish into thin air.
I just wanted to have some fun.
But you, oh you wanted to play games.
Fair enough, I thought and so I played along.
Such a soar loser you were, you called me names.
Bored me to death, you yourself burst your bubble.
The novelty wore off and it occured to me..
that you were nothing but a passer-by.

It felt calm, until it didn't.

Until your screams became a regular thing, that I woke up to
every morning,
And my so called dreams of us, turned into my worst nightmares.
You pissed me off.
So don't be mad at me,
For deep beneath, in the peat, is where you deserve to be.
Don't you complain, no no no...
Because you had a chance, yet wasted it as always.
You just have to be such a tease..
Well better luck next time, for now,

I wish, may your soul never rest in peace.

Sam's *POV* :-

I was at my house with my family. Suddenly the door bell rang and a tall blurry figure came in, uninvited. Then all of a sudden everyone started having lunch. The tall figure sat too. I couldn't make out who it was but I was acting as if I know that person. Out of the blue I shifted to a very dark and damp place. It was cold out there. Figuring out where exactly I am ; I saw the exact same tall and blurry figure approaching towards me. As it came more closer I could see it was a guy but his face was unclear. He tried to kiss me but I pushed him away. He forced himself onto me and I struggled to get those filthy hands off of me. I was sweating and panicking.

He said, "don't you want this now? Don't you want me now?" His angry voice gave me chills. I was disgusted by him, angry and afraid. I pushed him as hard as I could and ran away. I knew I was dreaming I knew this wasn't true . That this nightmare wasn't actually happening; but somehow I felt stuck and couldn't get out of that horrible experience. I kept running and my heart was throbbing out of pain. Suddenly I woke up. I was in my bed. I was panting and trying to catch my breath. "Phew, it was one hell of a nightmare.", I thought to myself. This nightmare got me thinking; and I realised something. Something very horrible. There was this guy, I call him myrtle now cause he's always whining about one or the other thing and also because he's dead to me. Myrtle and I dated a long time ago , in highschool. The whole time I was with him, it was an act of self destruction. I knew there was something not right about him; yet I kept ignoring the red flags. I now realise that the whole thing with myrtle affected me way more badly and I give it credits for.

Myrtle was tall not handsome and a hell lot of a mess. We met in highschool. He was persuasive , a smooth talker and thought he was funny; which was anything but true. He was those type of guys who say that there aren't like other people and then go to maximum heights proving themselves wrong by behaving the exact same way. Myrtle contradicted himself so much so that it was pathetic. He was manipulative, had anger issues and knew nothing about consent. It was my fault too that I was so naive and kept taking all his crap.

Myrtle tried to force himself on me once; kiss me without my permission. I kept pushing him away and he kept coming back; he finally stopped after I pushed him really hard . It felt like a nightmare and still haunts me sometimes. That is why I keep getting such horrendous dreams. Sometimes when bad things that happen to you, may it be big or small; conciously or unconsciously it affects you. It affects you a lot, until the extent of loosing your mind.

Consent is a very important thing in any kind of relationship. Whether you are dating, or married or just friends with benefits or anything else; it doesn't matter, because a 'no means no' It is not necessary that when someone denies you to do anything it has to be a 'no'. It can be a nod of disapproval, the other person telling you to stop , them saying no, pushing you away, etc etc.

One of the bravest things I have done in my life is standing up for myself and ending the toxic relationship with myrtle. I was brutal but I didn't care, because when it comes to your mental health and sanity; you should always be straightforward. Parting away from myrtle; I felt like I was breaking the shackles of grief, resentment and fear. Like I could breathe again. I did not shed a single tear, because I had cried rivers, when I was with him. In a hell hole. I learned a lot from my mistakes and now I know much better.

Many a times we choose to be with someone because we think we deserve it, that we deserve them because we think that we are not good enough for anything more. That's absolute crap. We are worthy of much more than we give us credits for. We deserve the best and should never settle for less.

✿ ✿ ✿

"The time you let your happiness depend on others accord Is when you loose it all.
You are in charge of your happiness and grief, the way you pursue things and the way you handle situations. The more optimistic perspective you have towards life is what makes you happier.
It's not the dreary clouds you should look at, but the silver lining."
"In all this chaos, when you feel that you need someone to be there for you; to hold you tight.
What you really need is a hug from you to yourself."

Standing up for ourselves is not easy. People can be manipulative and intimidating but at the end you have to do what's right for you.
Never settle for even the slightest bit of less, than what you deserve. You deserve all the good out there.

20. ~who am I ?

What I wanna be
[I pressed my nose on the window, as I gazed at the clouds with
curious eyes.
I was so fascinated by the view ; because I loved the high and
how tiny the world seemed beneath me.
That's when I told mom, as a five year old.
"Mom! I have decided! I wanna be a cloud when I grow up!"
"Oh really?? Wow that's, um that's amazing sweetie!", Mom said.
"I know! I can fly all day and..and can go wherever I want to. ",
I exclaimed.
"Sure", she said smiling; as she booped on my nose and kissed my
cheek.]

Well.. I clearly haven't become a cloud, so we can cross that off
the list. I won't stop trying though. Why am I like this?...oh don't
open that door.

1. Diary Entry-112 The Facade
I fear of losing myself in between all these masks that I put on for
various occasions. All these fake accords just to blend into some

social satires.. and what do I get in return? Nothing. The mask of "I'm okay", "I'm happy"...I shed it. It was hard, but once I took it off; it disappeared into thin air as if it never even existed before. Now all the hurdles, the battles of my own, the ghosts of the past and the thorns of my misery.. don't prick as much as they did before. I am not numb to the pain , but I am better prepared to let it heal through time. I don't hide it anymore, all the grief and the pain. I feel a lot , a lot of emotions. All of them go hand in hand but that just proves that I will have a emotionally rich life ahead. It's a handful I know, but it's better to feel something than nothing at all; because then you just exist.

"Times when you feel low
And you so don't wanna show
But you wish if they could know...
You just want that one person to come to you ,
All out of the blue...
And dance and sing
And add a little bling...
And hold your hand and look into your eyes
And say... it'll be okay."

2. Diary Entry - 209 :- Epiphany
Embrace the inner chaos
Appreciate the flaws
Knockdown the demons
Be an opportunist

Be eccentric
Live to the fullest
Before time deserts thee.
Most of the life's lessons; I learned them the hard way. The learning never stops though. The monogamy of life makes us believe that everyday seems the same nowadays. Is it though? Think again. Yes the sun always rises up the east but today it was a little different. It is a different hue of orange; the brightest shade from Van Gogh's palette. More vibrant than ever before, as if it glows with the passion of every young love that blooms in one's heart. Every sunrise is hits different...more beautiful and more serene than before. Each day the Willow sings me a different story, of bravery and wit and all the glory.
Diary Entry - 417:- The Hypothesis
I have always come up with the most uncanny yet interesting theories of my own. They define me in a way and I love how almost true they could be. Almost. One such unnerving thesis is the Multi-thesis.

• When one dies, there soul escapes neither to the heaven nor to the hell; but to a parallel universe through a void. The hypothetical multiverses is where the soul vanishes into. Your soul leaves your body and travels through a void entering yet another universe where it rejuvenates. The void erases all the memories of the past life and sets you off with a clean slate. Does that mean, all this time we try to escape/breakthrough one labyrinth, just to enter another? Maybe. The ghosts, the spirits or the unholy as some may call it are stuck in the same world even after dying,

because they have some unfinished business to do. One can pass through the void if only, they are truly satisfied with the lives they have led. Otherwise they wander in the nothingness. Those who are satisfied with their lives and yet are unable to enter the other universe ; become 'The Glitches in the Matrix.' Our entire existence is confined within a loop of such indefinite universes.

There is always room for such weird, mystical theories. One just needs to have the correct sense of mind for it. I am just a mere human being. We all are; but no one can exactly define us or pen us down on a piece of paper; because there is always more to you than you can ever imagine. The more you seek ,the more you find. I am my thoughts and my theories, my quotes and my poetries. I am you, and you and yes, you too; and I am me.

The Chaotic Peace

Life doesn't rhyme at every loose end.

There is a, b , a, b and there is a, b , c ,a.

We are always in the search of something,

In the want of something magical to happen to us,

To swept us off our feet and to make everything alright.

This magic that we want to happen in our lives,

It not necessary to be something out of a fantasy land...

We may find this magic in some place, someone, our sometimes, even ourselves.

Then we realise that we ourselves, are all that we ever wanted.

This sense of contentment gives us the sense of liberation.

www.ingramcontent.com/pod-product-compliance
Lightning Source LLC
Chambersburg PA
CBHW031338160726
47993CB00002B/740